BASKETBALL ★
How to Play the All-Star Way

by **Tom Withers**

Introduction by **Randy Ayers**

Illustrated by **Art Seiden**
Photographs by **Mary Pat Boron**

★ An **Arvid Knudsen** book ★

RSVP
RAINTREE
STECK-VAUGHN
PUBLISHERS
The Steck-Vaughn Company

Austin, Texas

Dedication

For my Mom and Dad with love and thanks.

Acknowledgments

Photographs from the collection of the Basketball Hall of Fame, pp. 6, 8, and 9: photographs from the collection of Madison Square Garden, pp. 14, 18, and 30: photographs from the collection of Robert Withers, pp. 24, and 27.
Photographs from the collection of Mary Pat Boron, pp. 4, 17, 26, 29, 40, 41, and 42.

© Copyright 1994, Steck-Vaughn Company

Published by Raintree/Steck-Vaughn Publishers, an imprint of Steck-Vaughn Company

Library of Congress Cataloging-in-Publication Data

Withers, Tom.
Basketball/written by Tom Withers.
p.   cm. — (How to play the all-star way)
"An Arvid Knudsen book."
ISBN 0-8114-5779-6 hardcover library binding
ISBN 0-8114-6342-7 softcover binding
1. Basketball—Juvenile literature. [1. Basketball.]
I. Title.
II. Series.
GV885.1.W57 1994
796.323—dc20   93-23275   CIP   AC

Printed and bound in the United States

2 3 4 5 6 7 8 9 0   99 98 97 96 95 94

CONTENTS

INTRODUCTION

I am truly flattered to be able to share a few words about a game that has influenced my growth and development in so many ways. Basketball was a means to an end for me. It provided me an opportunity to get a marketable education.

It was always impressed upon me to put the educational value of the game before the athletic. Discipline, hard work, team play, and setting and accomplishing goals are some of the many values that I have gained from the game. Isn't it ironic that these same values apply to personal and family life as well?

I hope, as you read the following pages, that you will also apply the fundamentals of the game to your life. I am convinced that they can have a positive affect on you!

—Randy Ayers
Men's Basketball Coach
Ohio State University

◀ Jumping for the ball under the net

Dr. James Naismith, the "Father of Basketball,"
invented the game in 1891.

IT STARTED WITH A PEACH BASKET

Basketball is a true, original American game. It was invented over 100 years ago by an American named James Naismith. Basketball has since become a popular sport all over the world. But basketball hasn't always been the exciting game you see on TV today. The rules and equipment of the game have undergone many changes. They happened long before Michael Jordan and his amazing slam dunks came along.

It was December 1891. The place was Springfield, Massachusetts. Dr. James Naismith, a YMCA physical education teacher, had a problem. Naismith's students had played football and soccer outdoors during the fall. But with winter coming, they would be forced indoors. Naismith wanted his students to have fun. He wanted them to stay in good physical condition. But he didn't have an indoor game for them to play.

One day, Naismith came up with an idea for a new game. First, he borrowed two peach baskets from the school's janitor. Then he attached them to the balcony at both ends of the school's gym. He then divided his class of 18 into two teams of 9. All he needed now was a ball. Naismith chose a soccer ball.

His students began playing by passing the ball around. Then they tried to throw the ball into one of the baskets. If the ball went in, 3 points were scored by that team. The students loved this new game! Naismith soon became known as "the Father of Basketball."

But Naismith's game still had a few problems. Every time one of the students made a basket, someone had to climb a ladder to get the ball. So holes were cut in the bottom of each basket. This helped speed up play.

A basketball game in 1892 using a peach basket and soccer ball

There was also no limit on how many players could play at one time. In one game at Cornell University, there were over 50 players on each team!

In early games, players had to sit in a penalty box when they made a foul. The penalty box was just like the one used in hockey.

Around 1900, the first real basketball was developed. In 1906, the peach baskets were gone. They had been replaced by metal hoops with backboards. More people heard of Naismith's new game. Basketball's popularity began to spread across the United States. It also began to look more like today's fast-paced game.

Senda Berenson, one among the first three women enshrined in the Basketball Hall of Fame, coached Smith College students in the first public women's game on March 22, 1893.

Through the 1920's and 1930's, the game continued to change. At one time, players could make passes by bouncing the ball off the side walls of the gym!

At first, basketball was played mostly in high schools and colleges. But by the 1940s, two professional leagues had formed. In 1949, the National Basketball Association (NBA) was created with eight teams. During the 1950s and 1960s, the NBA's best teams were the Minneapolis Lakers and the Boston Celtics. Both teams were led by star players. The Lakers had George Mikan. The Celtics had Bill Russell. In 1960, the Lakers moved to Los Angeles. The NBA grew with teams, from coast to coast.

One of the NBA's top stars in the 1960s and 1970s was Wilt Chamberlain. At seven feet one, Chamberlain could not be stopped. He led the league in scoring many times. He once scored 100 points in a single game!

By 1967, a new professional league, the American Basketball Association (ABA), had formed. This league only lasted until 1976. It had to fold because of money problems. Four of its teams then joined the NBA.

The ABA was known for its high-scoring games. The ABA used a red-white-and-blue basketball. Its star player was Julius "Dr. J" Erving. Erving was a six-feet-six showman. He could hold the ball in one hand and take off on his jump 15 feet from the basket. Then he would smoothly dunk the ball through the hoop.

The NBA teams became more popular than ever. More fans bought tickets to the games. Then the game became even more exciting in 1979. College superstars Earvin "Magic" Johnson and Larry Bird joined the league. Five years later, Michael Jordan entered. He took basketball to an even higher level of play. Jordan's super style of play has thrilled millions of fans all over the world. His love of the game shines through in every play.

Today, games are played on school playgrounds. People play them on home driveways. They are played in school gyms in every country. Boys and girls have discovered that basketball is a great way to make friends. It is good exercise, and it is fun.

Do you want to be another Michael Jordan? Do you want to try out for your school's team? If so, there are many places for you to play. Your school, city, or town may have organized leagues. Check with your local recreation department for information. Local youth organizations have excellent programs for players of all ages. The great thing about basketball, though, is that you don't need anyone else to practice. Just lace up your shoes, grab a ball, and have fun!

Dribbling down the court

CONDITIONING AND WARMING UP

Professional basketball players are among the most physically fit athletes. To get into good shape takes a lot of hard work. Good basketball fitness programs include many kinds of workouts. Running, jumping, and stretching are all very important. A healthy diet is important, too. Playing other sports also helps you develop skills. All these things will make you a better player.

During a basketball game, an NBA player may run 3 miles. You will not run nearly that far. But running is a key part of becoming a good player. Try some long-distance running. It helps build strength and endurance.

Swimming and bicycling are also great ways of improving your stamina. Danny Ainge of the Phoenix Suns swims 40 laps a day. He also bikes 10 or 15 miles several times a week. By improving your wind, you will play better. You will play as well at the end of the game as you did at the beginning.

You should also practice running short distances. Practice some starts and stops. Start and stop like you would in a game. A good basketball player moves well from side to side. A player must be able to move backward as well. Practice moving side to side and running backward. When running backward, try to stay up on your toes. Check behind you from time to time. Make sure there is not anyone in your way.

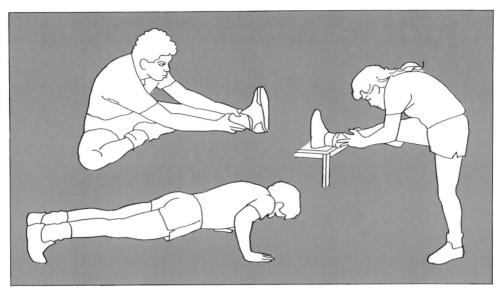

Stretching and conditioning exercises

Jumping is another skill you will need. You must be a good jumper to play well. The players who can jump the highest have a better chance of getting the ball. Improve your jumping skills by stretching. Jumping adds strength to your leg muscles. Good stretching will keep your muscles loose and flexible. This helps you avoid injuries.

Always take the time to warm up properly before practicing any skill. Your coach should lead you and your teammates in exercises. There are many stretching and warm-up exercises. Do them before a game or practice. You can also do toe touches, jumping jacks, and push-ups on your own.

Jumping rope is also a great way to warm up. It helps you stay fit. Try to stay on the balls of your feet when you jump rope. You will strengthen your calf muscles. Jumping rope can help you become a better jumper.

When working out, remember to start slowly. Do not overdo it. If you do not feel well, tell your parents or coach. If a muscle does not feel right, stop! Listen to your body. If something is not right, it will tell you. Playing when you are hurt will only make an injury worse.

Part of your overall fitness program should include a balanced and healthy diet. Eating some snacks is okay. Just do it in moderation. Nobody knows your body better than you. It's up to you to take good care of it.

Practicing setting up the shot

CHAPTER 3

YOUR EQUIPMENT

You need very little equipment to play basketball. With just a pair of running shoes and a ball, you are all set. Even if you don't have a basketball court nearby, you can still learn a lot about the game. You only need a ball and some room to bounce it.

Balls

Chances are you've played with a basketball before. You know they can be many different sizes. The ball used in many youth leagues measures 28 1/2 inches around. Girl's and women's teams use the same size ball. The regulation ball used in the NBA is 30 inches around. If you are a beginner, you may want to start out with a smaller ball. Your hands might not be big enough to handle the larger ball. That does not mean you cannot use the larger ball though.

There are leather covered balls made mainly for indoor use. There are all-purpose balls designed for use on all surfaces. It may be best to buy an all-purpose model so you can play on any court. A leather ball used outside on concrete gets scuffed up quickly. You will find a large selection of balls at sporting goods and department stores. They will range in price from $15 to $40. If you can afford it, it is helpful to have your own ball. That way you will not have to rely on friends. You can practice whenever you want. After you get your ball, it is a good idea to write your name on it with a magic marker. That way, if you lose it, you have a chance of getting it back.

◄ Scottie Pippen of the Chicago Bulls is considered
to be the NBA's best small forward.

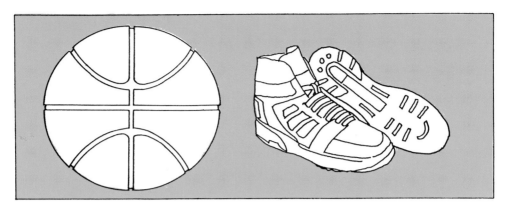

Basic equipment

Basketball Shoes

Basketball is a game that requires running, jumping, and pivoting. A player's basketball shoes are his or her most important piece of equipment. Basketball shoes continue to change. They now come in many shapes, styles, and colors. They can also range in price from $20 to $200! Some shoes are made just for basketball. Others can be used for many sports.

Some players may prefer a low-cut shoe. Others may choose to wear a high-top model. High-tops are very popular. They give your ankles more support.

In picking out a basketball shoe, make sure it fits your foot snugly. It should provide strong support to both your feet and your ankles. The salesperson should be helpful in finding you the correct shoe. Most of today's basketball shoes also have built-in cushioned arches. They give added support to the bottoms of your feet.

When trying on a pair of shoes, go for a test walk in them. Make sure they fit properly. You can even practice some of your basketball moves in them.

Socks

Choose socks that are comfortable. Because feet sweat, get absorbent cotton socks. Some players wear more than one pair of socks. It helps their shoes fit tighter.

Pads

For all its grace, basketball is a very physical sport. Sometimes there is hard contact. You may get some bumps and bruises. While not required, some younger players wear protective knee and elbow pads. The pads provide a cushion if you fall or dive for a loose ball.

Mouthpiece

More players at all playing levels are wearing mouthpieces or mouth guards. These protect your teeth and gums. Some youth leagues require you to use a mouth guard.

Offense and defense scramble for the ball.

PLAYING SKILLS

You have probably heard the saying, "Practice makes perfect." Well, nobody is perfect. All the practicing in the world will not make you a perfect player. But it will make you a better one.

Chris Mullin of the Golden State Warriors did not become an accurate outside shooter by accident. As a boy, Mullin spent a great deal of time practicing. He was called a "gym rat." He could be found practicing at any hour of the day. When he was in college, Mullin was given a key to the gym. That way he could practice any time he wanted. Mullin still shoots as many as 500 shots per day!

Fundamentals are the basic skills you will need to master to become a good player. The fundamentals of basketball are: dribbling, shooting, passing, and faking. These are some of the offensive skills you'll need to develop. Every player should be equally skilled at defense. Good defense requires balance as well as a desire to get the ball back for your team. The NBA stars have spent thousands of hours working on their fundamentals. You must work on fundamentals, too. Otherwise, you will never be an All-Star.

Basic Stance

On offense (with the ball) or defense (without the ball) you must learn a proper basketball stance. This is a position you can get into at any time. It allows you to always be ready for the game's action.

◄ Patrick Ewing, center for the New York Knicks and NBA All-Star, can do it all on offense and defense.

Your feet should be shoulder's width apart. Your knees should be slightly bent. Keep your back straight. Your head should be raised and your eyes alert. Raise your arms. Your elbows should be bent close to your body. Your hands should be open. Then you will be ready to catch or deflect a pass. If your hands are at your sides, you could miss a team-mate's pass. You could have a

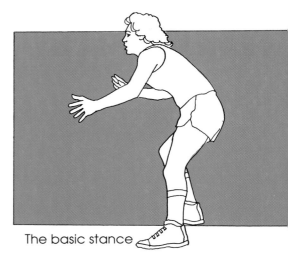

The basic stance

pass hit you in the head. Basketball is a game of nearly constant motion. This "ready" position will allow you to jump, or move sideways, forward, or backward instantly.

Pivot Foot

A pivot is the most fundamental offensive move. A pivot foot means that when you have the ball, you must keep one foot completely stationary. You move your other "free" foot. It is as if one foot is glued to the floor.

On offense, the player who has the ball cannot move both feet at the same time without dribbling. If the player does move both feet without dribbling, it is a violation called "traveling" or "walking." To move, the player will have to pivot.

To pivot, put your weight on the ball of one foot. Keep that foot in place. Move your other "free" foot in any direction. You can go in a complete circle as long as you keep the pivot foot in the same spot. But make sure you do not pick up or drag your pivot foot. If you do, you will be called for a violation. The other team will get the ball.

Dribbling

Many beginners do not spend enough time practicing their dribbling. They feel it is a very easy skill to learn. Whatever position you want to play, you need to dribble well. Becoming a strong dribbler will give you an advantage on the court. You can never be too good at dribbling. Some of the all-time best dribblers were NBA legends Bob Cousy, "Pistol" Pete Maravich, and Curly Neal of the Harlem Globetrotters. They were wizards with the basketball. They could dribble the ball between their legs and behind their backs.

Body Position

To dribble the ball, bend your knees, and keep your head up. Do not look at the ball. A round ball will bounce straight up into your hand after it hits the floor. Your head must be up when you dribble. Otherwise, you won't see what is going on elsewhere on the court. You may not see a defender coming at you. You may not see a teammate who is wide open.

Arm and Hand Positioning

Dribble with your strongest hand. Learn to dribble with your fingertips as much as possible. Try not to dribble with your palm. This may be difficult for younger players because their hands are not yet big enough. Keep your wrist and hand as relaxed as possible. Try to keep the ball under control. Imagine that the ball is attached to a string, like a yoyo. Try not to slap at the ball or tap it. Be as smooth as possible.

The protected dribble

Use your "off hand" (the one you're not dribbling with) to help you maintain balance. You can also use it as a shield against defenders. Keep your "off arm" close to your body. Keep it bent at the elbow. You cannot use it to "push" or block a defender. If you do, you will get called for a foul.

How to Practice Your Dribbling

Start in a standing "ready" position. Bounce the ball repeatedly in the same spot until you have the ball under control. Next, practice dribbling while walking. Start very slowly. Remember to keep your eyes ahead of you. Try not to look at the floor. If it is too hard to not look at the ball, practice in front of a floor-length mirror.

After you have some confidence, try some speed dribbling. Again, start in a good "ready" position with your knees bent. Keep your head up. Now, dribble the ball in front of you. Begin to jog forward slowly. Try to keep the ball close to your body. Concentrate on keeping your wrist and hand loose and your arm bent. Practice by jogging back and forth. Do this until you can complete two trips down the court without a mistake. Do it without looking at the ball.

Practice dribbling around some obstacles. Pretend the obstacles are defenders. A couple of chairs placed around the court can create a good course to dribble through. See how fast you can go through your course without making any errors. Confidence will come with practice.

As you become a better dribbler, you can then start switching the ball over to your other hand. This is called crossing your dribble. Every player should learn to be a skilled dribbler with either hand. This will make you a much more valuable player. You will be able to drive to the basket from anywhere on the court. A player that can only dribble with one hand is limited. He or she can be easily guarded because the defender knows which way that player is going to move.

Passing

Have you ever watched John Stockton of the Utah Jazz pass a ball? Have you ever seen Kenny Anderson of the New Jersey Nets lead the fast break? They are masters of the "no look" pass. They don't have to look around. They know who they want to pass to. When they pass to a teammate, it is an easy basket. Stockton has led the NBA in assists many times. Anderson is one of the game's rising stars. Stockton and Anderson are two of the best passers in basketball. This is not just because they are excellent at the skill itself. But they get as much pleasure seeing a teammate score as scoring a basket themselves. A good passer has to be unselfish. He or she should be willing to sacrifice his or her own point totals for a team's good. A good passer will help the team play as one by spreading the ball around to everyone.

Pass the ball with the fingertips.

There are many types of passes. Whatever pass you try, keep a few things in mind:

a) When dribbling, always pass by holding the ball with your fingertips. That way you will have control of the speed and the direction the ball travels.

b) Follow through after you let go of the ball. The completion of the pass is as important as the windup.

c) Keep your wrists loose and flexible. If you are too tight, you might throw a bad pass. You may lack the proper speed to get the ball to your teammate.

d) Try to lead your teammate with a pass. That means, try to throw the pass a little ahead of your teammate. Throw the ball in the direction he or she is going.

The type of pass you make will depend on the situation on the court. For example, if a teammate gets open for a lay-up, a long pass may be needed. If your team is setting up for a shot near the basket, you may need to bounce a pass to your teammate.

Here are a few basic passes you'll need to know. Master them to become an All-Star passer.

Chest Pass

The chest pass is the most fundamental pass. You will find it is the pass you use most. The pass should reach your teammate quickly. You should always try to get it to him or her at chest level.

A practice chest pass

Begin with a proper basketball stance. Line your feet up even with your shoulders. Keep your knees bent and your head up! Hold the ball in both hands with your fingers spread wide. Raise your arms to chest level. Keep your elbows slightly bent. Take a step forward in the direction you want the ball to go. Release the ball before your arms are fully extended. Do not forget to follow through. Follow through by snapping your wrists down so your fingers point downward. This will help you develop good passing habits.

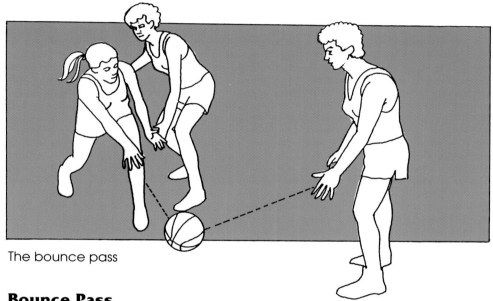

The bounce pass

Bounce Pass

The bounce pass is effective when you need to pass under a defender's reach. You do it almost the same way as a chest pass. Your arms should be reaching toward the floor after you let go of the ball. They should not be out in front of you. Aim toward a spot on the floor halfway between you and the intended ball receiver. Step forward and release the ball. Remember to practice the same follow-through you used when you made the chest pass. You should try to get the ball to your teammate above his or her waist. That way, the ball won't be grabbed by an opponent. Your teammate will be able to go into the next move.

The overhead pass

Overhead Pass

This pass is just what it sounds like. It is a pass thrown from above your head. It should arrive at your teammate's chest. You will see this pass most often when a player grabs a missed shot. The passer wants to get the ball up the court quickly. An overhead pass can be used anywhere on the floor. It is best when used to pass over the top of the defender.

Grip the ball on both sides with your thumbs pointing up. Keep your elbows and knees slightly bent as always. Raise the ball directly over your head. Step in the direction of the intended receiver. Then, bring the ball a little behind you. This will help to generate some power before bringing your arms forward.

Release the ball when your arms are almost fully extended. Snap your wrists as you let go of the ball. Again, make sure you follow through.

Baseball Pass

The baseball pass is used to throw the ball a long distance. It should look just like an outfielder throwing to a base.

Start by holding the ball in both hands. When you have found a teammate to pass to, bring the ball back with your strong arm. Hold it just behind your ear. If you have small hands, use your other hand to support the ball. Step toward your target. Release the ball as you step forward. Do not forget to snap your wrist. Follow through.

Throw this pass only if you are sure it will be caught by a teammate. You will also use it when time is running out. Use it when your team needs to move the ball down the court in a hurry. You have to be careful. The ball will be in the air for a few seconds. Defenders will have time to steal it.

You should practice passing drills with a friend. Even if no one is around to work out with you, you can practice in a school yard. Bounce passes off a wall or a handball court.

There are other passes you can try. But you have to be good at the basic ones. A behind-the-back pass and a no-look pass are fun to do. They are exciting for fans. But leave those to the pros for now. Work on your basics first.

The baseball pass

Catching

Players who have "good hands" catch the ball well. When you are on the court, you will have to be able to catch the ball. Catching comes before shooting or passing to teammates. It is important to work on your catching skills.

Always catch the ball with both hands. Keep your hands open wide. Keep your fingers spread apart. Never try to catch the ball with one hand! Players who try that usually drop the ball. They can't control it. Trying to catch the ball with one hand leads to turnovers.

Make yourself a good target for your teammates' passes. Work to get as open on the court as possible. Get into a good "ready" position before attempting to make a catch. As always, keep your knees bent in case the pass does not come right to you. You may have to spring for the ball.

Hold your arms at chest level. Keep your hands wide open. As the ball comes toward you, keep your palms cupped. This helps you to control the pass. Make your hands "soft" or relaxed before you receive the ball. Loose hands and fingers have much more control. You'll have less chance of "jamming" or breaking a finger.

Always step toward the pass. Watch the ball as it moves all the way into your hands. Do not stand still while waiting for the pass to arrive. Do not give the defender time to step in front of you. He or she will steal the ball.

You use the chest pass most to reach the catcher at chest level.

Faking is a move to fool the opponent.

Faking

Escaping a defender can sometimes be very difficult. To get free, or "open," you will have to make moves to fool your opponent. This is called faking. You can fake effectively with your feet, head, eyes, and shoulders.

To fake with your feet, shift your body weight to one side. Then take a step in one direction. As soon as you see the defender, step the same way, plant the foot you stepped with, and push off. Then step in a different direction. This is a useful move whether or not you have the ball.

A head fake works well when you are trying to attempt a shot. The defender is trying to guess your next move. A quick bob or jerk of your head might be enough to get your opponent to jump or turn the wrong way. A head fake is also helpful to get a defender to commit a foul.

Sometimes just looking in one direction and then darting in another will shake you free of the defense. If your first fake doesn't work, try something else. You will not do your team any good by standing around and watching. If you have seen Michael Jordan or Chris Mullin, they are always faking. They are looking for ways to get open. They want their teammates to pass the ball to them.

5

SHOOTING

The goal of every team on offense is to score. Putting the ball in the basket is every player's aim. Basketball is a high-scoring game. Players can score with a variety of shots. The lay-up or lay-in, hook, two-handed set shot, and jumper are the most popular shots. If you have watched or played, you have seen players try all these shots. You have probably seen other shots as well.

There are some things about shooting that you must know. For example, the power for your shot should always begin in your legs. It should flow up through your hips, body, arms, and hands. Finally, the power comes out through your fingertips. Your shooting arm should always be in a "cocked" position. This means the upper part of your shooting arm forms an *L* with your forearm.

Remember, even the best shooters make only about 50 percent of their shots. Do not be disappointed if you have trouble at first. Just keep practicing. By working on the basics, you will become a good shooter.

Shooting Stance

Your stance will be slightly different for each shot. But a good shooter always faces the basket before trying a shot. It is almost impossible to make a shot if you cannot see your target. You will sometimes hear this called "squaring up" to the basket.

◄ Michael Jordan was the most exciting scorer of all time.
He retired in 1993.

Always keep your knees slightly bent. It will help you maintain good balance. In case you miss the shot, you will be able to go after the loose ball or get back on defense.

Arm and Hand Positioning

Always hold the ball with both hands. That way it cannot be knocked away by a defender. Your shooting hand should be under the ball. Your wrist and hand should be cocked back toward your body. Your other hand should be on the side of the ball to use as a guide. After you release the ball, keep your arms extended.

Range

Range is the distance you are most comfortable shooting from. It is also the distance from which you can make most of your shots. Do not begin by shooting from 25 feet. Start from 5 feet away. Work your way out. Winning teams make most of their shots from in close to the basket.

Lay-up or Lay-in

The lay-up or lay-in is the easiest shot. This is because it is taken very close to the basket. The lay-up is usually made on the run. Most of the time it is banked in off the backboard. The lay-up is the first shot you should try to master.

Begin by practicing the lay-up from a stationary position. Stand to the right or left side of the basket. If you are right handed, start on the right. If your left hand is stronger, begin on the left.

From the right side, slightly bend your knees. Hold the ball in both hands. Take one step toward the basket with your left foot. Rise up onto your toes. Extend your right arm. Release the ball. Aim for a spot on the backboard where you want the ball to hit. If the ball doesn't go in, that is okay. Right now, pay attention to your footwork. Watch how you release the ball.

Soon you will be ready to try dribbling before shooting. Remember the dribbling skills we have already gone over. Start at a slow pace until you're able to make the shot over and over again. You don't have to be running as fast as you can.

The lay-up shot

Practice shooting the ball as gently as possible. Not every shot will go through the rim. After a while, you will begin to develop a "touch." Shots may fall through even though not made perfectly.

One-hand Set Shot

Start by facing the basket with your feet apart at shoulder width. Hold the ball in both hands. Keep it just below eye level. Do not hold the ball in front of your eyes. Bend your knees. Remember to draw the power for your shot from your legs. In one motion, rise up onto the balls of your feet. Extend your arms. Release the ball with your fingertips. Make sure you follow through. Some coaches tell players to aim for the front of the rim. Others say aim for the back. Pick whichever works for you.

Jump Shot

If you are a beginner, you may not be ready for the jump shot. Many younger players are just not strong enough. Jump shots take strength. You may not be able to shoot a jump shot. With experience and practice your jump shot will improve.

To take a jump shot, start by holding the ball with both hands. Like the other shots, keep one hand low and behind the ball. Your other hand should be on the side of the ball. Bend your knees slightly. Raise the ball as you begin your jump. As you rise off the floor, cock your arm in the shooting position. Release the ball by flicking your wrist as you reach the top of your jump.

Keep the elbow of your shooting arm tucked in close to your body. If your elbow "flys" out to the side, your shot will probably miss. As always, remember to follow through. Extend your shooting arm and hand as far as you can.

The jump shot is hard to defend. Practice this shot from different angles. Try shots facing the front of the basket. Try shots from the sides also. Use the backboard to bank in your shot.

Hook Shot

Kareem Abdul-Jabbar was the all-time greatest scorer in pro basketball history. He was the master of the hook shot. Abdul-Jabbar is seven feet two. When he took the hook shot, it was called the "sky hook." Your shot will be much closer to the ground than the sky. But the hook shot can still be a good offensive weapon. It does not matter even if you are only four feet tall.

The hook shot should be taken within 15 feet of the basket. That way your chance of making the shot will be greater. Do not try your hook shots from 30 feet away. You will probably not make the basket. It may also get you benched by the coach.

Players often shoot the hook shot after getting the ball near the basket. After catching the ball, take a step toward the basket. Extend the shooting arm away from the body. Flick the ball toward the rim. You may not have enough wrist strength to flick the ball. It is okay to use more arm strength to get the ball above the rim.

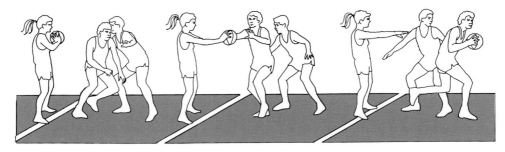

The throw-in

CHAPTER 6

THE GAME OF BASKETBALL

To play basketball you need to know the rules. Players who do not know the rules make fouls or violations. This can cost their team a win. It is a good idea to get a basketball rule book. That way you can add to your knowledge of the game. You can get a rule book at your school. Ask at your library for one.

The Court

Basketball is played on a court. The indoor court usually has a hardwood surface. The outdoor court has an asphalt or concrete surface. The size of the court may vary depending on the size of the gym. It can vary with the level of basketball you're playing. Professional and college courts are 94 feet long and 50 feet wide. Most high school courts are a little smaller. The courts used by most youth leagues are even smaller.

The long lines of the court are called sidelines. The short lines are called end lines or baselines. Most courts have two circles in the middle of the court: a center circle four feet in diameter and a larger one 12 feet in diameter.

At both ends of the court are backboards. They are either made of wood or clear plexiglass. The baskets are attached to them. The shape of the backboards can be a rectangle or fan. You may sometimes hear the backboards called the "glass."

The basket or rim is attached to the backboard exactly 10 feet above the floor. Some schools' gyms and some playgrounds have baskets lower than 10 feet. But most league games are played with

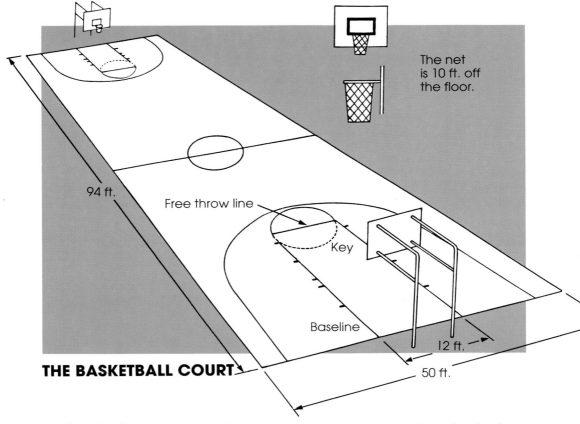

The net is 10 ft. off the floor.

94 ft.

Free throw line

Key

Baseline

12 ft.

50 ft.

THE BASKETBALL COURT

10-foot-high baskets. A nylon or cotton net is attached to the basket. The net hangs below the rim.

There are two lines extending from each baseline toward the center of the court that come together in a half circle 19 feet from the basket. Inside, these lines form the key or free throw lane. The key is 12 feet wide. It is a restricted area. The key is the area extending from the baseline to the top of the free throw circle. During a game, any offensive player can be in the lane for only three seconds at one time before being called for a violation.

Referees

There are usually two referees in any basketball game. The NBA and major college basketball games use three referees. The referee's job is to see that the players and coaches play by the rules. The referee is the boss on the court. What he or she says is law.

Fouls

The referee can call two types of fouls. They are personal fouls and technical fouls. A personal foul is called against a player making illegal contact with a player from the other team. A technical foul is called when a player or coach curses or argues with the referees. Technical fouls can also be called if a player tries to enter the game before the referee "whistles" them in.

Violations

The referee will blow his or her whistle if a rule is broken. This is called a violation. The team that made the violation has to give the ball to the other team. Traveling (walking), three seconds in the lane, palming (carrying), and double dribble are some of the most common violations.

Time

How long a game is depends on who is playing. In professional leagues, games are divided into four 12-minute quarters. College games are split into two 20-minute halves. High school games are usually made up of four 8-minute periods. Most youth league games are made up of four 6-minute quarters.

There is usually a 2-to-3 minute break between quarters. And there is at least a 10-minute intermission at halftime. During these breaks, players can get a drink of water and rest. Their coaches can discuss new strategies.

If two teams are tied when time runs out, an overtime or extra period is played. In the NBA and in college games, teams will play a 5-minute overtime. Youth leagues use 3-minute overtime periods to decide a winner. If the teams are still tied following overtime, they keep playing until there is a winner.

Scoring

There are two ways to score points. Scoring is done by making field goals or free throws (foul shots). A field goal is any shot that goes through the basket. A free throw is a free shot. It is awarded to a player who has been fouled by another player.

If a player makes a field goal, 2 points are awarded to his or her team. A team gets 3 points if the shot is made from beyond the 3-point line. The 3-point line is a line drawn on the floor extending from the free throw lane. The distance of that line from the basket varies from league to league.

Free throws are worth 1 point. They are shot from the free throw line, which is 15 feet from the basket. A player is awarded free throws after he or she is fouled. Free throws are also taken after a technical foul has been called.

Starts and Stops

Every basketball game begins with a jump ball at center court. The jump takes place between one player from each team. The teams will usually send out their tallest players. But sometimes a team sends its best jumper to win the tap. The referee tosses the ball straight up. Each player will try to tip the ball to a teammate.

Basketball is a fast moving game. The only stops occur when the period ends and when the referee blows the whistle. The referee blows the whistle when there is a foul or a violation. The game also stops if the ball goes out-of-bounds.

Basketball is a fast moving game.

CHAPTER

7

YOUR TEAM

For a game to begin, both teams will send 5 players each onto the court. Each team has a center, two forwards, and two guards. The position you play will be based on your team's needs. If you are tall, your coach may ask you to play center. It will not matter that you may want to be a point guard. The position you play may also change as you grow. It is a good idea to learn to play all the positions. This will make you a better all-around player. It will make you more valuable to your team.

Some of the best players in the history of the game, like Magic Johnson and Larry Bird, were great at any position. They worked on their basic skills. They had the desire to be All-Stars.

The Center

The center is usually a team's tallest player. Because he or she is shooting at a goal that is 10 feet high, the closer a player is to the basket, the easier it may be for him or her to score. That does not mean that player is the best player on the team, however.

A good center should be able to score and rebound. A center must be good at blocking shots. Rebounding is getting the ball back for your team after a shot has been tried and missed. Centers should also be good passers. A team often passes the ball to their center when they first get the ball over center court. The center should then pass to a teammate who is open for a shot.

NBA All-Stars, like Patrick Ewing, David Robinson, and Shaquille O'Neal, are all more than seven feet tall. But they are able to do many of the things shorter and smaller players can do. They can dribble and shoot like guards. That is because they practiced their basic skills.

When a team has the ball, that team is on offense. A team's center will often play with his back to the basket. It makes it easier for his or her team to pass the ball. A center playing close to the basket on

Offense charging up the court

offense is playing in the "low post." Other times, the center may move out toward the foul line. This is called playing the "high post." To be an All-Star center, practice your skills inside the foul lane. Centers who "wander" outside of the lane may get in their teammates' way. They upset the offense.

If you are tall, make the most of it. When you get the ball on offense, keep it raised. Keep the ball at chest level or above your head. By dribbling, you'll take away your size advantage. You give opponents a better chance of stealing the ball.

If a team is not on offense, it is on defense. It is trying to prevent the other team from scoring. It is the center's job on defense to control the area close to the basket. The center will have to guard his or her opponent. The center rebounds missed shots. He or she blocks passing lanes. This is done by getting in a good position to act in the lane. Defensive play by a center takes lots of hustle.

The Forwards

The forwards play the baseline and the foul lane. They play along with the center. Sometimes, a forward may play the outer limits of the foul lane with the guards. An All-Star forward must be a super passer, dribbler, and shooter.

◄ Getting the rebound

In the NBA, you may hear about two forward positions. They are the power forward and the small forward. A power forward usually has a larger build than a small forward. He or she is counted on by the team to do more rebounding. A small forward is shorter and quicker than a power forward. The small forward may do more scoring and outside shooting.

Karl Malone of the Utah Jazz is the leading power forward in the NBA today. He was nicknamed "The Mailman" in college. He always delivered for his team. Malone can rebound and score. He always makes it tough for his opponents to play. They do not score a lot against him. Malone plays a very physical style of basketball. He uses his wide body to "box out" opponents. That means he positions himself between the ball and the player he is guarding. In this way he can get to the ball first. Malone is also a top outside shooter for a player his size. Malone said his shooting "touch" came about by practicing many hours as a boy. His family could not afford a basketball hoop. So Malone hooked a wire to a tree in his backyard. He would practice shooting for hours.

Scottie Pippen of the Chicago Bulls is thought to be the NBA's best small forward. In the NBA a six-feet-seven player is called small! Pippen really stands out as an athlete. His speed lets him get away

from players who try to guard him. He is also one of the best jumpers in the league.

Frontline players, such as a center or a forward, on offense have to set screens for the team. This is done by blocking a defender's path. In this way a teammate can get open to receive a pass or take a shot.

The Guards

A team's two guards form the backcourt. Guards need to be very good dribblers and passers. It is their job on offense to bring the ball up the court. Then they pass it to an open teammate.

The point guard is the team's playmaker. He or she is like the quarterback on a football team. It is the point guard's job to direct the offense. Sometimes a point guard will drive to the basket. This is to create an opening for his or her teammates. That is why a point guard should be a good dribbler. The point guard has to be aware of where his or her teammates are. The point guard must know where the defense is. It is a big job.

Magic Johnson was one of basketball's all-time greatest point guards. He led the Los Angeles Lakers to five NBA titles. Johnson could dribble around and through tough defenses. He made perfect passes to his teammates.

The off guard or shooting guard is the team's best outside shooter. Shooting guards often place themselves on the outside edge of the foul lane to shoot.

The Coach

The coach is the man or woman who runs the team. The coach may be a teacher or a teammate's mom or dad. It is up to the coach to make the team into a unit. The coach has to plan which 5 players to put on the court. The coach has to decide which positions they should play. It is not an easy job!

The coach has to deal with the team's many people. He or she has to help them improve their different skills. Listen to your coach. Do not be afraid to ask him or her for advice and help.

◄ Defense blocking his opponent

DEFENSE

In a game, every player on the floor will play on offense and on defense. To be a complete, all-around player, you must spend half your time working on your defensive skills. The other half is for your offensive game. Michael Jordan is great not only because he is the NBA's top scorer. He is also one of the league's best defenders.

Your main goal on defense is to stop the other team from scoring. You cannot stop them every time. But by playing good defense, you can cause them to try harder shots.

The basic defensive stance is much like the one you use on offense. Your feet should be shoulder width apart. One foot should be a little in front of the other. Bend your knees. Raise off your heels onto the balls of your feet. Your arms should be raised above your waist. They should be ready to defend against a pass, shot, or dribble. Keep your elbows slightly bent. Make sure your hands are open with fingers apart. This stance allows you to move where the offensive player goes.

Your feet are your best weapons on defense. Move by using a sliding, side-to-side shuffle step. As the offensive player moves, you should, too. Many players who are out of position try to make up ground. They will reach out at an offensive player and be called for

Team defense , a necessary skill

a foul. This is because they didn't use their feet. Never cross over your feet. This will tangle you up. The offensive player will be able to get past you.

Always concentrate on keeping yourself between your opponent and the basket. Stay about an arm's length away from the person you're guarding. But do not touch him or her. Of course, there's going to be some contact. But you cannot grab or hold an offensive player. The NBA allows its players to hand check (touch a dribbler once in a while). Hand checking is against the rules in all other leagues.

Look at a player's midsection when you're playing defense. As we discussed, a player will try to fake you out with his or her arms and legs. Keep your eyes centered on the player's stomach.

It is very important to stay alert. Keep active on defense. Move your feet and move your arms. Hustle to get the ball back so your team can score.

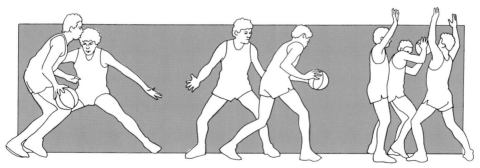

Defensive positions

Being a Team Player

There is nothing worse than a poor sport. Being a gracious winner is important. Do not pout when you lose. Do not blame a loss on your teammates or the referees. Show respect to your coach and to your teammates. Respect the referees and the other team.

In a game, some players may "trash talk." They will want to rattle you. It is okay to have fun and kid around with each other. But you should never make fun of an opponent. Never use profanity. It may be hard at times to ignore teasing. Concentrate on playing hard. Be the best player you can be. It's great to become a skillful player. But you will have to mix your skills with the skills of other players.

A team's goal is to win. To win, each player must place the team's success ahead of his or her personal glory. Everyone wants to be the one to score the game-winning basket. But it takes equal efforts from everyone for a team to win.

Part of being an All-Star on the court is acting grown up. Set a good example for younger players. After you have played, shake hands with your teammates and opponents. Being a good sport will win you friends. Then you will be a player everyone likes on and off the court.

GLOSSARY

Backboard: The board behind the basket

Basket: The metal hoop or goal (rim); also a score when the ball goes through the hoop

Box-out: When one player puts himself in front of the other player to stop him or her from getting the ball

Double-team: To guard one offensive player with two defenders

Dribble: To move the ball around the court by bouncing it

Field goal: A shot taken from anywhere on the court; also a basket

Foul: When a player makes illegal contact with an opposing player

Foul lane: The area between the free throw line and the basket

Free throw: An unchallenged shot that is worth one point; also called a foul shot

Free throw circle: The circular area surrounding the free throw line

Free throw line: The line showing where the free throw may be attempted

Hand check: When a defensive player lightly touches an offensive player with his hand

High post: The area around the free throw line

Hoops: A slang term for basketball

Jump ball: When a referee tosses the ball in the air between two opposing players

Jumper: A shot attempted by shooting while jumping

Key: The area extending from the baseline to the top of the free throw circle

Lane: *See* foul lane

Lay-up or Lay-in: A shot taken close to the basket

Low post: The area near the basket

Mid-court: The center area of the court

Palming: An illegal method of dribbling the ball when a player uses a palm to get under or scoop the ball before dribbling it

Personal foul: A foul called on a player

Pivot: A method of turning on one foot; also refers to the center position

Rebound: Any missed shot that bounces off the basket or backboard; to grab a missed shot

Screen: A stationary position an offensive player will use to block a defensive player so a teammate can get open

Set Shot: A shot taken while standing still

Tap: *See* jump ball

3-point shot: A shot attempted from outside the 3-point line which is worth three points if made

3-second violation: When a player is called for being in the foul lane for 3 seconds or more

Traveling: Taking more than one step while having the ball; also called walking or steps

Turnover: When the offensive team commits an infraction causing the other team to gain possession

Violation: An infraction of the rules that is not a foul

FURTHER READING

Antonacci, Robert J. *Basketball for Young Champions.* McGraw-Hill, 1979

Burnet, Chris and McSweeny, Sean. *Step-by-Step Basketball.* Gallery Books, 1990

Duden, Jane & Osberg, Susan. *Basketball.* Macmillan, 1991

Gutman, Bill. *Basketball.* Marshall Cavendish, 1990

Jacobs, A.G. *Basketball in Pictures.* Putnam, 1989

Rosenthal, Bert. *Basketball.* Childrens, 1983

INDEX